Ignited Lines

Meena Chopra

———————————

Collection of Poems with Drawings

Publisher: StarBuzz Media, Canada

ISBN No : 978-0-9813562-4-2
© Meena Chopra

Ignited Lines II edition. : 2010
First published in 1996

Publishers : **StarBuzz Media Canada**
1022 Zanre Crescent Mississauga
Mississauga, ON. Canada
L5J 4M8
starbuzz.ca@gmail.com

Price : 12.00

Painting on cover and inside drawings are by the author.and art.

Cover Painting "Adrift" with Air India in their art collection

"....Painting and poems go very well together. There is vitality in the forms, colours and the words chosen by Meena Chopra. Here is a charming feast of lyricism in paintings and poems."
- Late Dr. L.M. Singhvi
(These comments were left by him in my Visitor's Book, during my art exhibition and launch of 1st edition of 'Ignited Lines' in London U.K. 1996)

Reviews-

"Meena Chopra will not have too many words getting in between the ignition of an idea and its consummation. It must be having to do with the fact that she also paints. Her poems have neat compactness of paintings; words become colours that fill up the canvas if-or when she is not using her brush. Ignited Lines, Meena's first volume of verse, is therefore not for the gallery; rather, it is a gallery. You can browse through it, but you will periodically pause, much like when confronted with a new painting that has succeeded in achieving the different, a range and depth of emotions far removed from the every day clichés of existential dilemmas, not existence. She unveils shimmering facets of love, possession, mind and self with sensitivity. She is delicate but strong, gentle yet sharp, vulnerable yet proud. Self-actualization is more a matter of routine than effort; it is the moment beyond the ones of self knowledge that she wants to live up to, and become, not a mere rhapsody in search of life but a rhapsody in search of the deeper self. In this sense she is her own Sun, her own guiding star as is brightly revealed in the poem 'Fire'."
Gautam Siddharth   The Pioneer (Book reviews), Delhi, (India) 28.9.1996

"Accompanying the cluster of these lovely oil pastels worked out like 'two inches of ivory' are her versus. The words and the visuals support each other and the viewer is taken on to a journey to the end of the clouds. Look at her art or read her poetry there is a feeling of scaling heights, going to the mist of the mountains and scenting the fragrant pines."
-Nirupama Dutt   Indian Express (India), August 22 1999

"Each one of the forty expressions picturise a lived reality, an

*experienced emotion, a missed heartbeat without being senti-
mental about it. Nothing comes as after thought or an over-
statement. She is precise and matter of fact even in articula-
tions .....*
- Suresh Kohli   The Hindu, Delhi, (India)1.12 1996

*"These poems talk of 'hidden fire/rising with/a smoky
thread.....' A seemingly ordinary enough statement, it might
also mirror the extraordinary sensibility of a committed artist.*
-Adrian Khare   Blitz, Bombay, India 13.3 1993

*"...by one who is also an artist, a painter, provides perhaps an
alternative and additional medium of self expression to a sur-
charged personality. It is the story of a soul that is caught in
the throes of trying to unravel the mystery of the self in terms of
subjective experience. "*
*- Dr. Shalini Sikka, The Weekend Observer (Review) Delhi(India)
January 4 1997*

*"A characteristic of her style is that physical sensations beauti-
fully blend with abstract thought – yearning for fulfillment is
attended upon by consciousness of fragmentation."*
- Dr. Shalini Sikka   The Quest, Ranchi (India) 1996

*"Ignited Lines, a collection of poems by Meena Chopra, ex-
presses desire for ignition of the mind for illumination in a
world of duality and paradoxes."*
*- Dr. Shalini Sikka   The Journal Of The Poetry Society
(India), 1996*

*"Images have been made use of in abundance while expressing her
feelings, thoughts and views .... The poems are short but very pow-
erful and impressive indeed! Meena strikes with force to show her
caliber of thinking which is on par with any Indian modern poet
who is of great repute."*
*- M. Fakhruddin   Poets International, Banglore, (India) De-
cember 1996*

"Meena Chopra's poetry mirrors her acute sensibilities which, in turn, enmesh with her deft strokes on canvas."
- S. Rajoo   *The Times of India, Delhi, 23. 7. 1996*

"In paintings there is a poetic beauty and poems are strong in imagery and spontaneity. And both types of work are intense in movement"
- Deshbandhu Singh   *Rashtriya Sahara, Delhi, (India) August 1996*

"Her works are the rhythmic expression of the state of the sub-conscious. "Sparkling vacuum that glimmers and floats in the morning breeze...." Or   "A chilly winter blossoming in spring..."
 - Soumik Mukhopadhyaya *-The Statesman,   Delhi, (India) 20th August 1999*

"The embryonic bond that she shares with nature forms the key-note of her work. My feet stick to the damp earth / Fearing devastation / My mouth is full of clay / Is it the smell of the soil that I eat?/ Swallowing every bit. Words freeze the impalpable fears finding their refuge in the womb of earth. And the pastels accompanying the words, capture the anonymous smell in a tensile cage that bears the colour of earth. The other elements of nature find beautiful expressions in her works. Swirling flames of orange recalling to protecting warmth and destroying the fury of fire. Ice blue serenity of water... And most of all, it is the interaction with her own self that gets portrayed in her works."
- Critic   *First City, Delhi, (India) August 1999*

"Accompanying her paintings are her verses, and the two compliment each other. In Fact, they often seem to flow from and into each other, making one wonder which came first, the word or the image. The heightened passionate quality of her verses imbues the images with a strong emotional power"
Manisha Vardhan   The Pioneer, New Delhi(India) August 11 1999

"One notices a rhythm of universal duality underlying her poet-

ry as well as her paintings. The poems strong in imagery and spontaneity complement the paintings"
- Critic   First City Magazine, January 1997

"What ever the reason, there is no doubt that this lady packs a lot of talent. To be a mistress of words and lines is no means a feat by any standards."
- Critic   Financial Express(India) July 21 1996

"What adds to her talent is the beautiful poetry she writes... Her verses at times influence her paintings and vice versa."
- Akshaya Mukul   The Pioneer, Delhi, India, June 13, 1996

"Paintings and poems by Meena Chopra at the Jehangir Art Gallery, turned out to be a veritable feast to the eyes as one drifts from spasms of energy thrust into the portrait to the lovely exterior.
- Venkastesh Raghavan   Free Press Journal , Bombay, (India) 11th March 1993

"The book 'Ignited Lines' thus presents a deep insight into the inner passages of delicate human emotions and inner meanings .... It is a beautiful example of simplicity and feeling embedded together, obviously by a very talented writer.. The poems, on the whole are charming pieces of more finished art which have surpassed the realms of literature because of embellishingly philosophizing of the subject"
- A.H. Naqawi   Day After , Delhi, (India) 30th Sept.-14th Oct. 1996

"Her canvasses have fluid grace and character that is reflected in her persona too. Her paintings are as intense as the poetry she writes".
-Anshu Khanna   Savvy (India) 1992

"...for she does succeed to a remarkable extent in self-expression. Her thoughts, aspirations struggle and internal conflicts find faithful reflection in her works".
-V.V. Prasad   MID-DAY (India) December 9, 1986

Contents

Contents

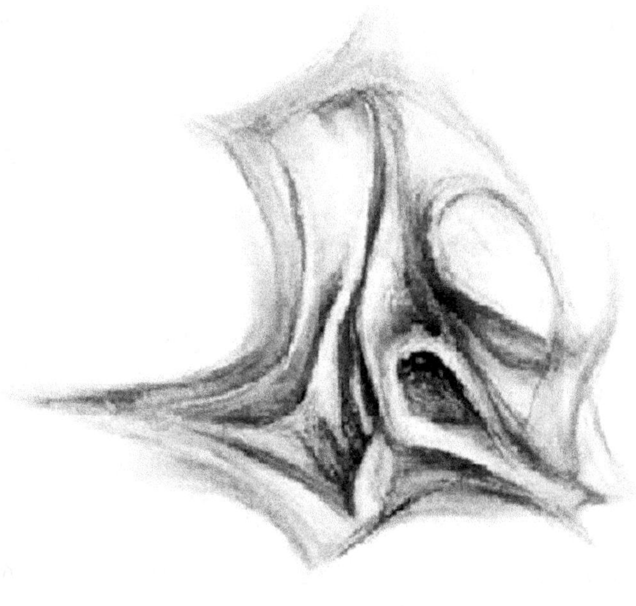

To Bhupinder and Taabeer

My poems search for the universal duality, a relationship between the subject and the object, spirit and the matter, trying to find the totality in this influx of paradoxes, in an effort to unlock the mysteries of life. I search the elusive reality of human consciousness through the lines, splashes of colors and the impressions of brush strokes on my canvasses and at times through pen and paper in the form verses.

First edition of this book was published in 1996. The overwhelming response from the readers of these poems from all over the world made me work on the II nd Edition . I am really thankful to all to give me this encouragement to come out with this collection again. In this edition some of my drawings have also been added and are in juxtaposition with my poems. I have added eight new poems as well.

I have also started trans-creating these poems into Hindi language. I would love to share these with you in future. I have trans - created one and added it at the end of the book.

- Meena Chopra

ACKNOWLEDGEMENTS

I would like to thank all the well wishers and friends for their support and encouragement for bringing out the second edition of this book.

I extend my special thanks to
Mr. Keshav Malik - Poet and Art Critic (India)
Dr. Kailash Vajpeyi - Poet an Philosopher (India)
Mr. Jatin Das—Artist (India)
Mr. Keki Daruwalla - Poet (India)
Dr. Shalini Sikka - Professor, English Literature (India)
Mr. H.K. Kaul - Poet (India)
Ms. Marian Kutarna - Art and History department, Mississauga Library (Canada)
Mr. Bhupinder Virdi - Life Partner
Ms. Taabeer Virdi - Daughter

I

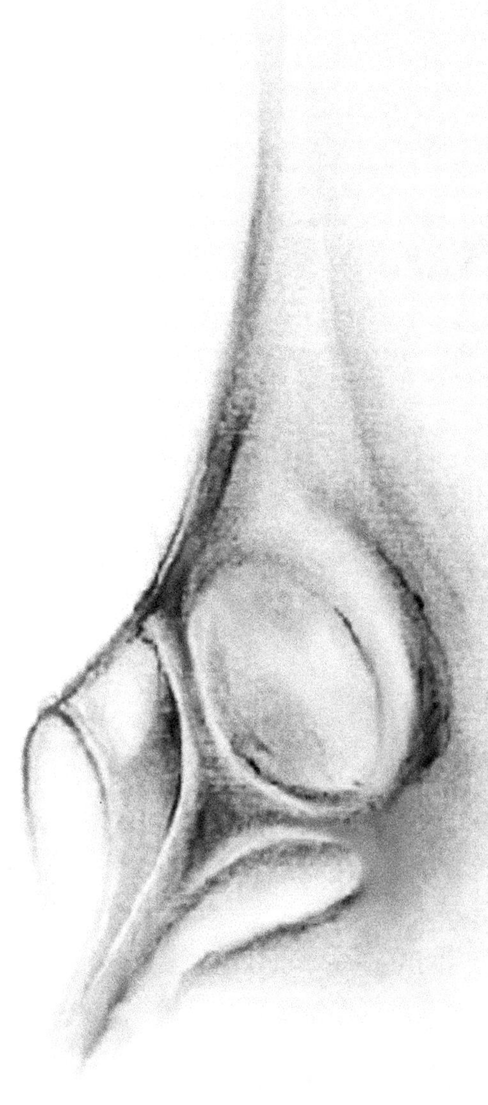

White Canvas

Your vivid stroke
etched in my memory
bestirred my stark white canvas.
A passing night clasped me
replete with colours.
Raw impulses wide awake
splashed shades
tinting the sheet
toning the moods.

A splendor bedded
with me all night.

A river
oozed out in heat.
My opaque vision.
grasped the forthcoming dawn.
A fatigue
tarried within me
throughout the day.

Metaphorical

Separated
from the start
I longed to be with you.
Submerged in a silent moment.
But it was the void
that greeted me,
not you.

Emptiness all over.

Nothing satiated.
Nothing fulfilled.
Naked sensibilities
cried out
unheard
torn apart
seeking a touch
your warmth ?
Estranged -
slept a restless slumber
failed to enter
my arid blank body.
Alone
distanced
unfamiliar shadows
lingered between us.

The want in me to see
the stark reality,

my untouched clear reflection
in your searching eyes
met despair.
Unrecognized, helpless and dirty
I hid my self from me.

Strange it is,
desire that breathes life
disappears
afraid of being alive.

I did not look
for a metaphorical love
not anymore

Never.

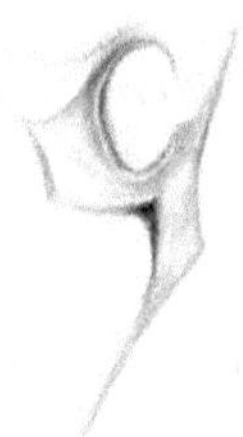

A Death, A Begining

Have you ever searched?
Your lost self
unfolding those
ruthless cold nights
inside me - ?

Ever dreamt?
The blazing honesty of
my unyielding
unborn
unprotected
vulnerable naked - self
in your arms,
enslaved
in disastrous fantasies,
tearing me apart
making me a whole
grasping a moment
beyond bondages,
seizing
a death
a beginning
an eternal embrace
unraveling mysteries
unknown - ?

Have you ever discovered,
worshipped,
my primeval existence
within you?
Recognizing
loving
the woman in me!

Strangers

In the day's heat
I sought myself in you.
Strangers we were, still are
silhouettes in each other's eyes.
Remnants of a deflected time.
Monotony
Nonexistence is
claustrophobic.

I fear remaining an outline.

Your warmth lingers
uncaptured,
fading into opacity.

I know 1 will burn
till the fire burns in me.

Ignited Lines

Sensitive fingers
touched the soft mud
igniting the lines
in my palm.
Sun's brittle brightness falls,
earth evaporates
in a thin layer,
glazing a clear sky.

Aghast I am !
My flesh tingles.
A restlessness
empowers me
wanting the mud
once again
in a tight grip.

My fingers tremble
drinking the soothing vapours
emitted from the impressions
carved on my hands.

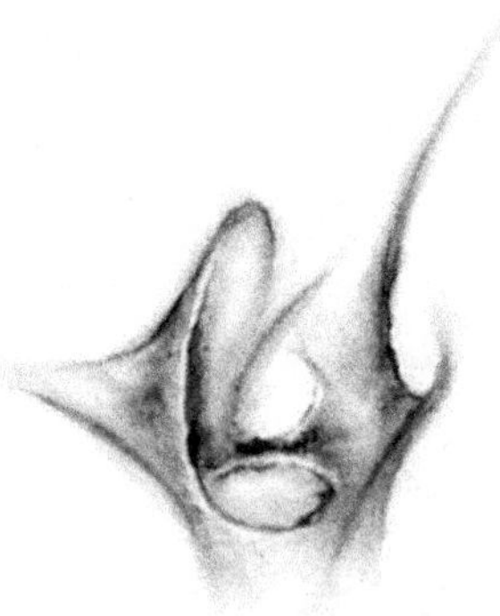

Adrift

A bright sunshine
smiles
surfs
the shores of horizon.
A sparkled vacuum glimmers
floats in the morning breeze,
trickles down
in the thin lines of my palm.

Trembling fingers,
reach out
seeking
a fragrant dawn
concealing a universe
stroking the innermost
mingling with the blood stream
savouring
fullness from my lips.

A twinkling moment
adrift on your body,
a spotless undiluted soul
surfaced
ceased
to be my being
forever.

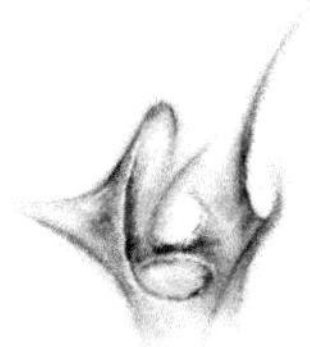

Unbound

My vision
seized
your distinct fragrance
searching a nucleus
into the sky's core.

Silent,
dimly perceiving
tender sensibilities
your dissembled thoughts;
distort them not
with the touch of
stoic hands.

A timeless moment of love
let it remain that--
pristine
unrelated
unbound
to figures and names.

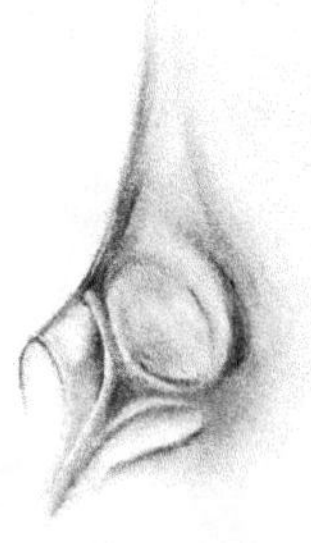

Iconoclast

Is she a vase,
a statue on a pedestal ?

She is no icon!

Her feet strong
firm on ground.
The earth supports her.
The real in her
longs to be
revealed through layers
seeking identifications
undraped
in a figureless
formless existence.

In vain,
she searches - an iconoclast,
beyond the turbidity of love.

Will she find one in you ?

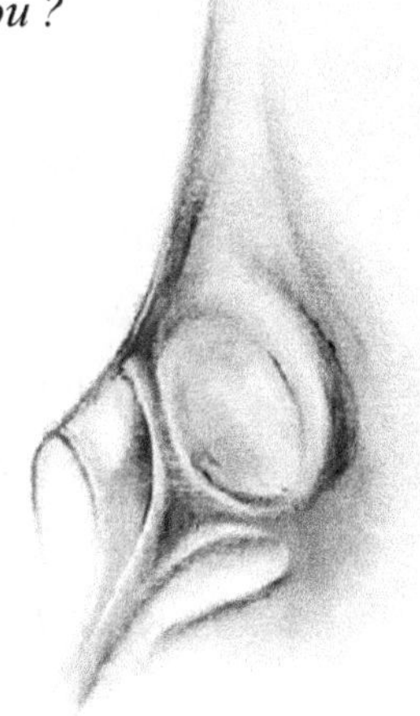

A Glimmer It Was

A glimmer it was--
was it you
or the sun ?

A chilly winter
blossomed in spring.
Whiffs of the flowers fled,
diffused in the sky.
The rainbow emerged,
half born,
half engulfed,
wonder-struck visions stopped
at the semi-circle.

Near was the horizon
distant was - I.
Closed eyes captured
unfolding emotions
but
the feelings
flowing and flying
endeavouring to touch
the rainbow,
plunging in space
searching
the elusive pot.

Is it the treasure ?
Will I find
my lost destiny there
with you beside me ?

A destiny-
lost in our hearts
at a time
when the time was
Stillborn.

A Stillness Moves

Distances fade,
a feeling
as if 1 touched
the limitless remains.
Quivering fingers
grasp the floating clouds.
They merge in me
as I in you.

The hues of blue
disappear
in each other,
when the sky
re-emerges,
beneath to above
getting wet
by the fresh rain.

My feet soaked
embedded in sand
leave impressions
strong enough
wiping off
the tidal waves
    that strike
    the climax within.

Sand slips away
under my feet.
A stillness moves
inside me.

Duality will remain
I know,
separating me from you,
yet a dream is instilled,
I pulsate
yearn--
to be fecundated
by the distant you.

(Poem got honourable mention from
Mississauga Library System)

When Labour Comes

*Your seed
in my depths
impregnating
preserved
miscarriages
not any more*

*only chance
surrender
to your strength
will be mine*

when labour comes.

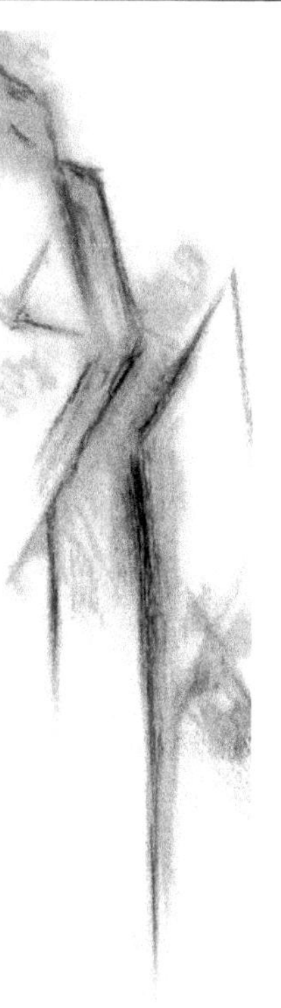

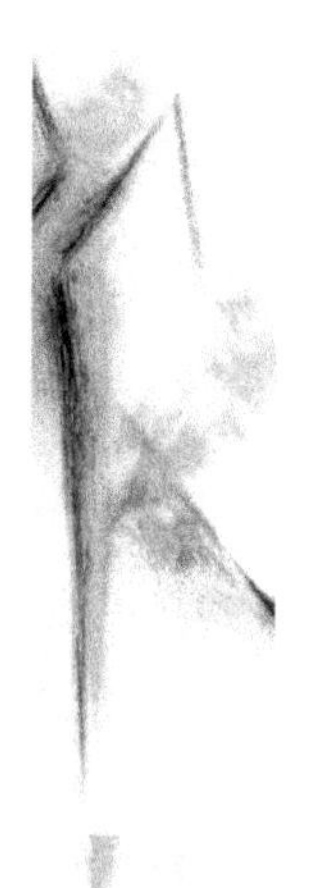

Haze of Dust

Will you share

the ashes of the burns ?

Feel what I yearn

with the eyes

of your fingers

before it mingles

with the haze

of dust.

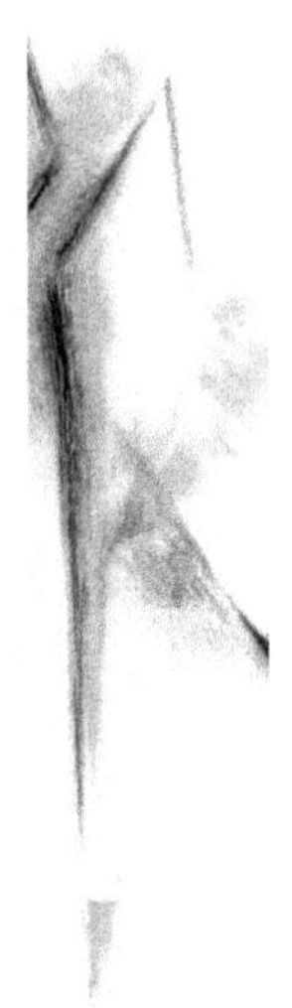

If I See

No,

do not touch the ash!

It still cries,

yearning with the residues

of fading embers.

My heart will bleed

even further

if I see

the spot of a burn

on your

loving fingers.

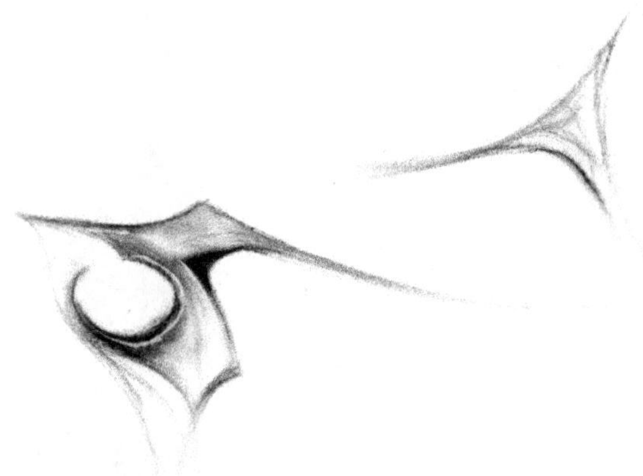

Whirlpool

Whirlpool
of soundlessness.
A plunge
to reach
the core of you,
the core in me
churns
frailing parts of
my body.
Small fragments floating
in turbulence!

But dear,
an agony it is
not getting to you.

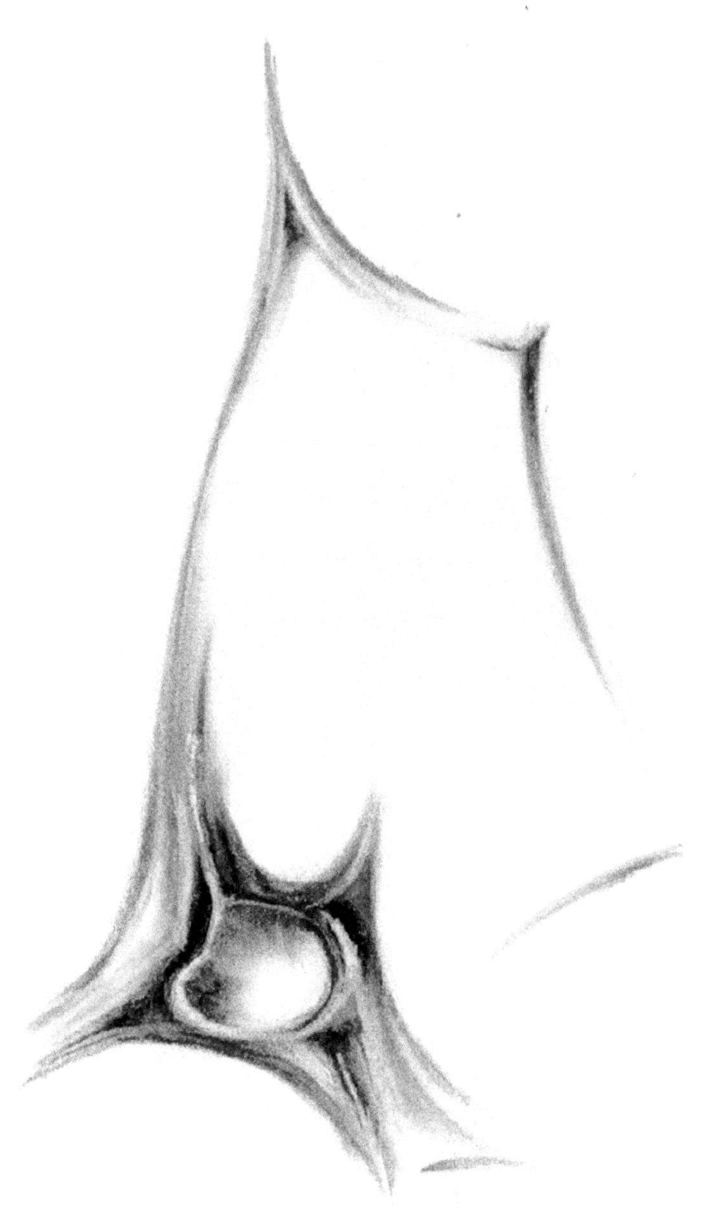

II

Centre-Point

Penetrating

mute stones

frozen hearts

leave impressions

expressed

in the arena

a lifetime

searching a stir

a centre-point

from where

it all began.

Instant In Motion

Trimmings

old and torn

change in

the flowing stress,

a garb,

hard cover,

hiding an instant

to be touched

to be in motion.

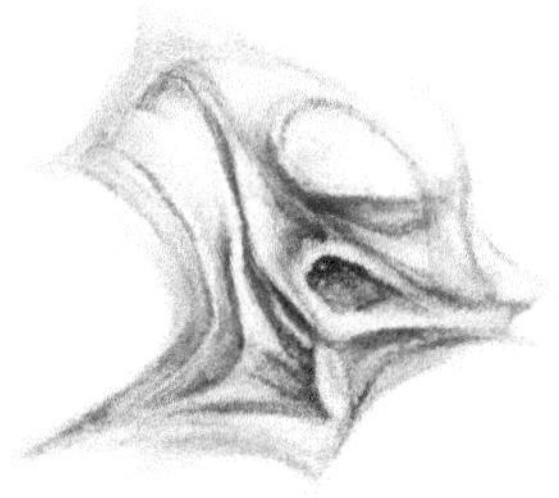

What Was It

Graying evening.

Shades of black fading.

Starkness of night!

Neutrality spread

all over our faces.

Unrecognizable!

What was it?

You recognized

I did not!

Was my vision Hazy,

or I looked at the haze?

Perhaps

we are beginning

a new end.

Paradox

Shadows from the past

spill into the future

the present,

a maze.

Unawareness sprawls.

Tired hands grope

for the rudiments,

fragmented,

flamed desires,

breaking the barriers,

the power

binding our separateness,

seeking totality

within a paradox.

Seeking Stability

Precarious moves.

A groundless stability.

Submerged pictures

of pathetic serenity.

A profuse desire

to follow -

the laughable stock,

disintegrated diffusion.

A firmness of cynical mind.

The dawn breaks

with the disappearing gloom

of a restraining sunset.

Potency

Thoughts immersed verses.

A rhythmic fantasy.

Pondering in the mortal failure;

bursting shadows,

a lifeless poise-

potent enough to unite

the clinging poverty

of a sterile substance.

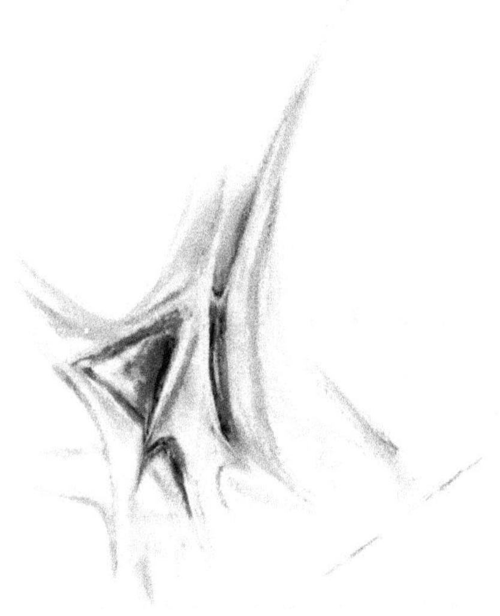

What If-?

My lap extends.

My belly encircles

the limits of the sky.

What if

the belly retracts!

Extensions lost!

Will these stars

remain

or fly away ?

Only chance

to hold them

tightly,

not relieving them.

But my body is

empty again ?

Aroma

Piercing stones

drop in a flow of

flying feelings,

trying to find

fearlessness

in the fluid

that churns and mixes

speeding moments

that static stillness

of loud trumpets.

The refined starkness,

authenticity,

falling throughout

the aroma of universality.

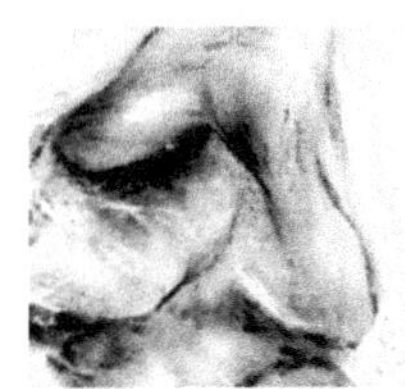

Memories

All the stars

engulfed in silence

trying to grab

the hands of futility.

The day explodes.

Whiteness spills

the residues of

the waning moon.

Death of the night

is still alive

in the memories of space.

Fire

Dreams

tumble from

unknown heights

into a dark pit

devoured by

the hunger for light.

A vast ultimate

flux of shadows

adrift

a sea of

hidden fire,

rises with

a smoky thread

to reach

the hearts of

early desires.

The Sleep of A Rising Day

The diffusion of silence.

Deadly!

Moments of passion

break into shreds,

fused together

sparkle smile of an ocean,

submerged

deep into the recesses of

hidden hearts,

where nothingness

can reach

to wake

the sleep of

a rising day.

Lunar Circle

Strolling thoughts -

spring in the sounds

of bewilderment,

strike the fullness

of the lunar circle.

Days diminish

in a friendship

of articulate silence.

Life begins,

understands meanings.

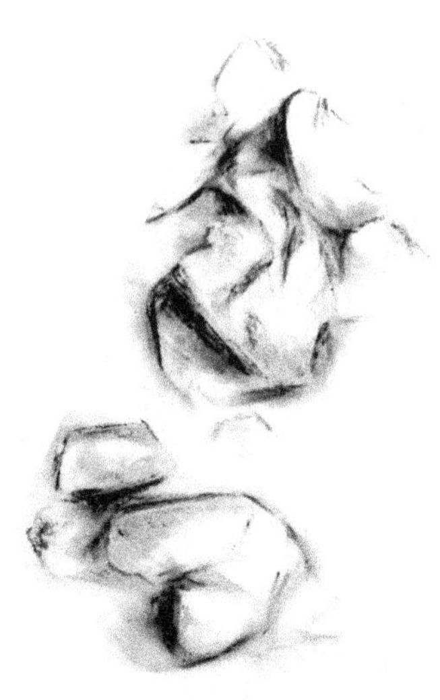

Ingle

A point of climax.

Clamorous roads.

Divided passions

sliding down

a roaring sea.

Drenched perspirations

wavy impressions

the calmness of moods

subdued.

Where's the ingle?

That kindled in a corner

long ago.

III

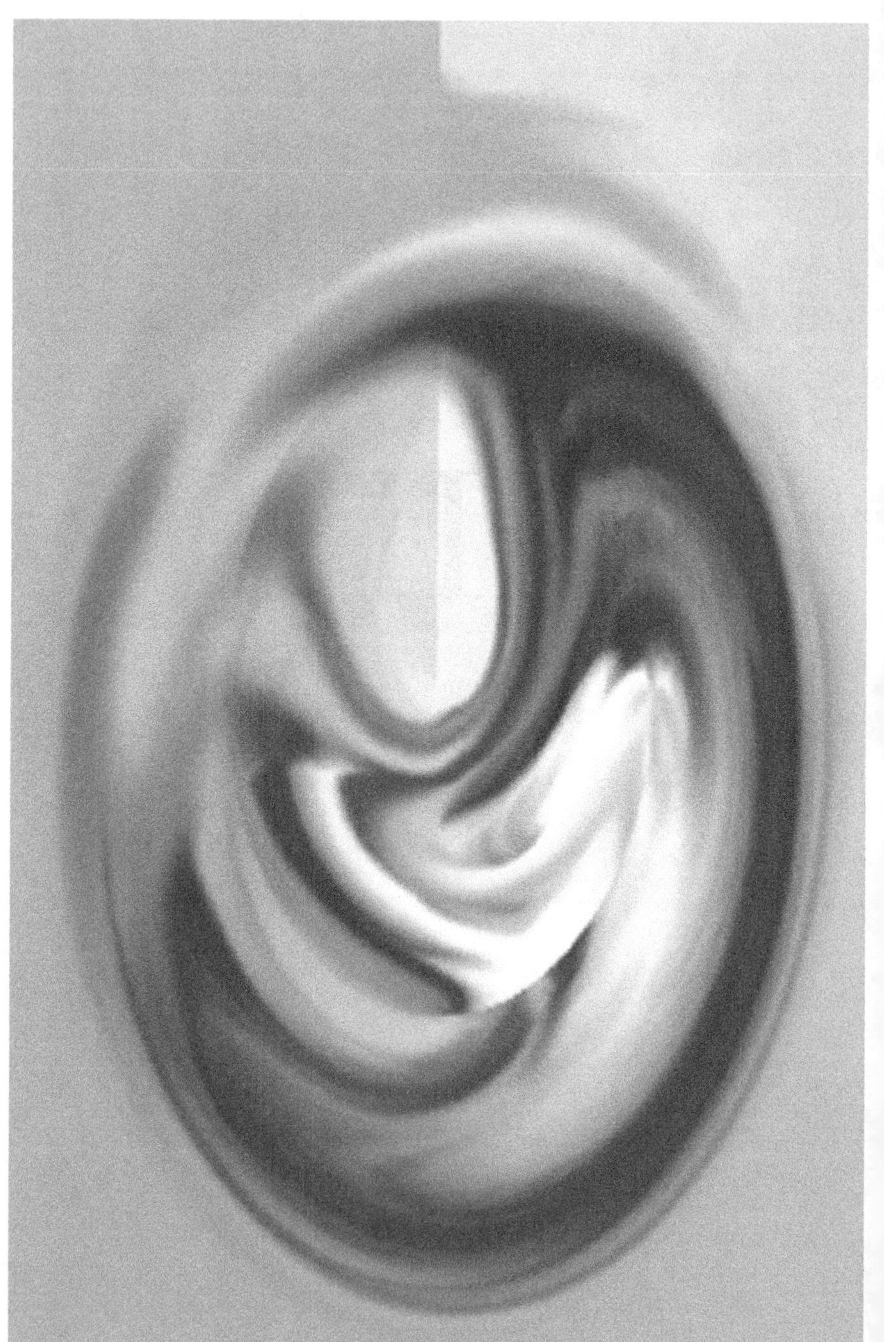

Zygotic Stupor

A dot she were,

her being

a zygotic stupor--

a peaceful sleep in

the mother's dark womb.

She raged to grow

splitting into several,

multiplying a

schizophrenic metamorphosis

from an embryo to a foetus.

Ready for birth

into a space of chaotic movement.

Coming to terms with what ?

Evolution ?

A dawn- ?

Ashes!

Frozen into embers

fall from the dust of smoky clouds,

liquefying the moments

into the deep sleep

of a crying earth.

Warming its core

sprouting in flowers,

spreading a ray

of dancing music

in the obscure corners

of dark rooms.

Illuminating what

a dawn - ?

Last of Ash

Summer heat walks.

Burning roads of death.

Passion of noon time.

Piercing rays of

the sizzling sun.

There are no flames

no figures and names.

An invisible touch

burns the body

to nothing.

Perhaps

the last of ash!

Ruins

I walk bare feet

on the ruins of time.

Past crumbles underneath.

Images emerge

from the rigid stonewalls.

Cracking in front of me.

I see shadows

in the debris of

empty spaces.

Pyre

Vanishing traces
Burnt desires
Shred a turning point.
The ruins of despair
remain.

A thread
A smoke
breaks the intimacy
with the scotched fire,
rises,
seeks the evening breeze,
an echoing silence.
invisibility
disappears in the furor--
Is it my pyre ?

Unending Point

Thunderous tones.
A fine thread of
lightning flashes.
Skylessness emerges,
ruptured by
an unending point
of disaster.

The day lapsed
became
a magic in the music,
churning
vibrating hearts
old enough
to be dust,
cramped in the sky
with limitless agonies
of human desires.

Hot Day

The hot day
passed on
a story to
the approaching night.

The eyes of sleep
searching
the blood of heat
of the innocent
shed during the day.

A restlessness
looks for the reasons,
a tranquility
reaching hearts,
so that
it sleeps
in peace
for a while.

Tangled in Time.

Dissembled thoughts
Barricades,
Past, Present, Future
Dusty.

Symbols dissolve
for me to plunge back
float and delve.

But, I stick to the moist damp earth
fearing devastation.

My mouth is
full of clay.

Is it the smell of the soil that I eat?
The dry coarse earth?
Is that me?

The streams swim in my eyes.
Visions divide .
The sight freezes in the silent snow.
Cold wind hovers
tangled in time.

Lost Paradise

I saw the landscapes.
The dead ages,
the ones yet to come
through the thinning mists.
Blending and bending
a patterned present.

Is this the fulcrum?

Is this the voyage?
I sought in the moments of love?
Or is it a vision,
deathlessness?
Still-
Clinging, confining to the outer -
The shell remained hard,
unperceived.
prison windows closed.

I inhaled your body.
It remained in me forever.
Inhalations and exhalations
looked for a breather in you.
Sensations lit a flame.
A ceaseless rhythm.
Waves pulsated,
A fire,
surging desire,

an unknown paradise.
I resolved in you for a while.
But
A cold black flame,
burnt within
I clawed the air,
grabbed the emptiness
clutching
a dim memory,
a distant past.
Light and shades
created my worlds
then, and even now.
I longed for the essence
a distilled clarity,
crystalline brightness,
a magical metaphor,
an unknown world.

Is this the fulcrum?
Is this where I will find
my lost paradise?

Deleted

We moved from dissonance to consonance
a final note of
harmonic progressions.
A rhythm of an unknown melody was being
substituted by a poetic syllable.

But all was deleted in one stoical stroke.
Effaced from the memory stick.

Was that a tainted time?
Consumed!
In a soft data
of a timeless zone?

An undefined me?

Not computed.
beyond calculations.
Separated from the
compounds and constituents.
Searching the light.
Photographic expressions.
Imaging -
The unresolved?

Entwined Dimensions

Unravelled mysteries
coloured wide spaces
entwining dimensions.
The vacuum
became horizontal.
Lines deciphered.
Core looked for its periphery
having fallen out
of the centre.

Searching?
The centre
or the periphery?

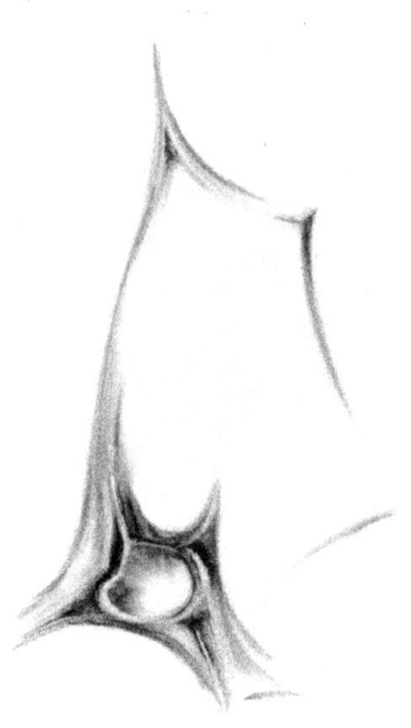

Flicker

Particles of a shivering flicker -

a tangible smoothness

tries getting into

the essentials.

An inactive gravity

stops suddenly

hesitating perhaps

unaware of the potentialities

it has to light the warmth,

a summer in the passing phase

of severe winter.

Mysteries

Colours

mixed,

soiled to

a dirty mud

finding

sparkling

globules of sunshine,

descending from

the smiling sea of

the sky.

Seeking a shore

in the mysteries

of the horizon.

Search

A room

full of tumbling noises

bouncing wall to wall

within the unventilated

bricks.

Unbearable.

Unknown footsteps tres-

passed.

Strangeness came over

creating a hollow.

Space entered

the dimensionless existence

beginning a new journey.

An unknown

unabated search.

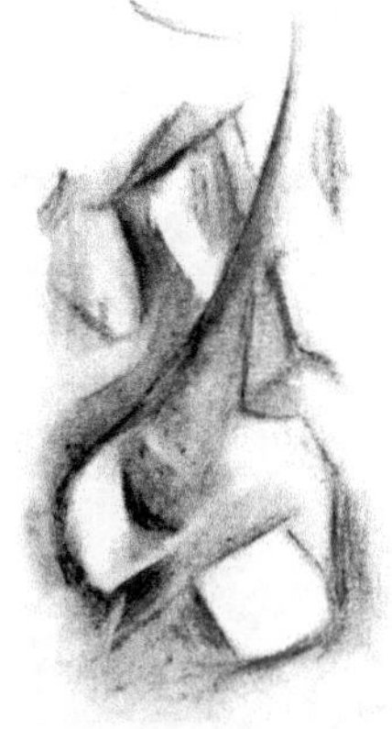

Sleep

My feet

gripped a panorama,

searching for roots,

for heat in each atom.

A split source,

schismatic agony,

birth

filling life with

an elusive glow.

The foundations walk away,

I run after them

without let!

My unfixed gaze

loses the range

where a breathless seed

delved in a sleep.

Future

The rain savoured the grounds

of Nainital

I stepped out,

a sultry morning glazed me.

I stared at the passing time

Taabeer—my little daughter

held me tightly.

I heard her say—

Ma, "where the hell are you?"

Can I have a Pepsi?

My little flesh was

wrapped in the

future of plastic water.

Setting Sun

My feet deep in sand

watched the sprawling sea

A setting sun.

Mist covered me

smooching the shores.

Lush green jungles behind me

I breathed a complete silence.

The twilight watched me

spilling out behind

the dark glasses of the clouds.

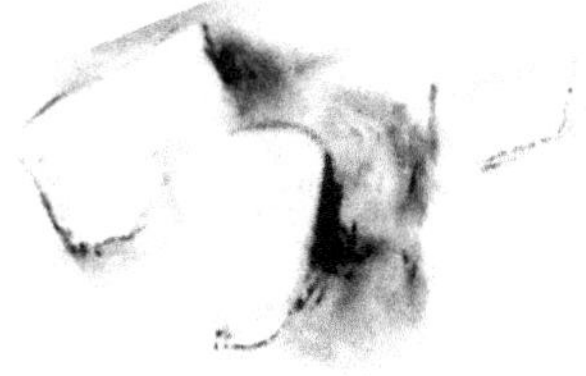

Entranced!

A sketch on my body and flesh

rhymed an oceanic silence.

Entwined in one breath

Spaces fell out

Entranced!!

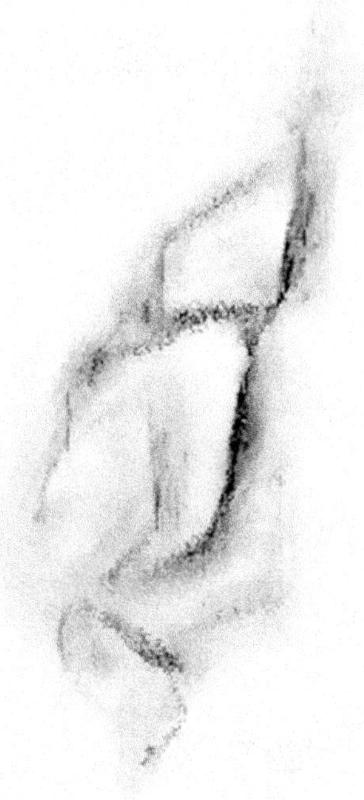

Reverberations

The thrills masquerade
even as they experience
a world of expansion.

Far away,
I shrink in a black hole,
where life searches
for the charismatic remote leisure,
seeking a strength
as I stand
face to face
with the deserted truth.
A plunging darkness
as bare as death,
where a dot
disperses a line
in a voluminous circle,
folding the fire
of a living time.
Images annihilate.
The body-less voice prevails.

What was it
that whispered-
reverberations in a chilled silence.

Splinters

She sprang a full swing.
Her hands itched
capturing the moon -
a snowy darkness.

She opened her fist
to a forthcoming dawn,
showing off
the precious possession
she owned.

Amazed,
she found
stained splinters
a broken glass
whiteness
drenched in blood.
A torn palm.

She looked up
beyond the transcending dusk,
the orb still alive
lit the heaven
spreading a borrowed light.

Fragility

Dancing on the shaky floors

of fragile buildings.

Piercing voices

lifeless faces

externalized

floating

breathing the heat

having it neat

hoping for what-

emancipation ?

What was It?

Graying evening.
Shades of black fading.
Starkness of night!
Neutrality spread
All over our faces.
Unrecognizable.

What was it?

You recognized
I did not?
Was my vision hazy?
Or I looked at the haze?
Perhaps
We are beginning
a new end.

क्या था वह?

सिलेटी शाम के

ढलते रंग

निःशब्द, निशाचरी, निरी रात

उदासीन, तठस्थ सफेद चेहरे

अपरिचित नाम

अनजान शब्द

खड़े थे रूबरू हमारे।

क्या था वह —?

शायद कोई अनुनाद —?

जिसे तुम छू भर कर निकल गए

और मैं देख भी न पाई।

कोलाहल की धूल से भरी

इन आँखों में

केवल थी तो कालिख ही

शोर की धुन्ध हमें टिकटिकी लगाये

लगातार देखती थी।

शायद एक शुरूआत के छोर पर

खड़े होकर हम

दूर किसी अंत को समेटते हुए

फिर एक बार

एक नई आस के करीब

बना रहे थे

एक नया सा नसीब।

Ignited Lines

Meena Chopra:
(Author, Artist,   Artist Educator, Community Work in Arts, Art Curator Advertising, Media, Broadcasting)

Art: Meena Chopra is an internationally known visual artist & poet with an unbridled passion for space, colours, forms and words.. Born and brought up in Nainital, a Himalayan hill resort of Northen India, now lives in Mississauga, Canada. Meena graduated in science from Isabella Thoburn College, Lucknow, India. Later qualified as a designer in 1977 from Delhi India and as an Artist Educator from RCM Ontario in 2009. After having a career as a designer for seven years with a couple of leading garment firms of New Delhi India, she later switched to fine arts, simultaneously pursuing her career in marketing and advertising as an entrepreneur. Primarily a self taught artist, she informally got trained and mentored under master artists at Triveni Kala Sangam, New Delhi, where she took visual art and sculpture classes. She has been professionally practicing fine arts since 1985 till date and writing poetry from 1992.

She has held several art exhibitions in India, Canada, England, USA and has over 70 group and solo art exhibitions to her credit. Some of these include premier art galleries like *Jehangir Art Gallery Bombay, Shridharani Gallery New Delhi, Triveni Gallery New Delhi, Nehru Centre London England, Art Junction New Delhi, India Habitat Centre, Jain Marunouchi Art Gallery USA and New Delhi, Gallery Aurobindo New Delhi, Design Exchange Toronto, Streetsville Gallery, Mississauga, Heritage Mississauga, Central Library Mississauga. Living Arts Centre.etc.* She was invited by 'Mississauga Arts Council' to put up a solo art exhibition "Culture Days Doors Open celebrations" at *Sampradaya Art Creations* in 2014. Many group art shows have also been curated and designed by her.
Her art and poetry has been extensively critiqued and reviewed by some of the well-known art critics/journalist writers of India, Canada and USA.

Her paintings are with many Corporations, Government Bodies, Embassies, Hotels and Private Collections in India, Canada, Australia, England, Switzerland, Dubai and Kuwait.

Author/Poetry: She writes both in English and her native language Hindi and has authored two poetry books. She co-edited a Hindi and Urdu e-poetry anthology RANG AUR NOOR (Colour and Radiance) in 2014, of the poets residing in Canada . Link: http://issuu.com/starbuzzcanada/docs/rang_aur_noor11_july_24_300_1_ . Her poems and articles have been published in many national and international journals.

Community Work In Arts: Meena is passionately involved in community arts with a motto of *"bringing the diverse communities & cultures together onto a common platform through arts".* She has been on the volunteer board of many arts and community organizations and has chaired many art and cultural events. She represented Canada and also India in many art and literary international conferences and events.

She has also conducted art workshops for Peel Board Schools, Mississauga library, art galleries and for some not for profit organizations. She specializes in MANDALA art workshops involving seniors, adults and children as meditative and therapeutic practices She also has been teaching art to special needs kids. These days she is engaged in teaching art to special need adults at Pixie Blue Studio at Port Credit, Mississauga She has been the director/owner of LEARNA HEARTLAND EDUCATION CENTRE in Mississauga since 2006 to 2012 .

Along with her artistic career she has been an enthusiastic Advertising, Marketing & Media professional with an intensive brand building experience of over 20 years. Launched and started Bhumeeka Advertising (New Delhi, India) in 1985 and ran it till 2004 while migrating to Canada. As an advertising and marketing professional she has worked with diverse ethnicities, multicultural markets & communities.

She has also been a producer and a host of a popular musical, ethnic radio program "Radio Shehnai" at 1320 AM in Canada (2012 to 2013). She has been a publisher of a popular ethnic entertainment newspaper called "StarBuzz" since 2007 . These days she is involved in making of a TV program called "EK NAZAR" (A Glimpse). This program's aim is to bring out and discuss the 'elemental poetic quality' of popular Hindi film songs so that they can be the subject of serious study.

BLOGGING ACTIVITIES:

Hindi blog: http://prajwalitkaun.blogspot.ca

English Blog: http://ignitedlines.blogspot.ca
General Blog: http://meenasartworld.blogspot.ca

Honours and Accolades :
- Meena has been recipient of first prize by 'Visual Arts Mississauga' celebrating 150 years of Canada in 2017.
- She was been awarded with prestigious "Mahadevi Varma International honour" for her contribution to literature and arts in 2018 as a litterateur and artist of Indian origin residing outside India
- She received Honourable Mention at Poetry Writing Contest 2003 held by the Mississauga Library System, Canada.
- She was nominated for "MARTY'S Awards" for literature in Mississauga 2010.
- She was awarded "Build India Award" by Bharat Nirman, India for artistic achievements outside India in 2015.
- She was awarded for 'Artistic and Literary' works by ICACI (Indo Canadian Arts and Culture Initiative of Canada) on their 4th Annual Celebrating Womanhood Gala 2016.

- She was awarded as Face of India in Canada by Colours of India, Canada for her artistic contributions while bringing the communities together, 2014.
- She has been honoured for 'Outstanding Service and Commitment to Diversity and Inclusiveness' from Peel Community Connections, Canadian recognition of her contribution to the 'Unity in Diversity' in 2006.
- Meena Chopra has been acknowledged and recognized for her work in the "community development" through her art, poetry and community work by Hon`ble Jason Kenney, the then Minister of Citizenship, Immigration and Multiculturalism in 2010.
- She was also recognized by Member of Parliament Mr Navdeep Bains, MP, as a "powerful bridge builder in 2010".
- She has also been recognized as "woman hero" by World Women Global Council for her contribution in the community 2013.
- She has been nominated for "THE CREDITS" by Heritage Mississauga for community work 2014.

Website: www.meenachopra-artist.com

Comments by some International Poets and poetry Lovers on the poems in English.

"I first read Meena's works here, at 'Post Poems'. I was intrigued by the vivid imagery portrayed in her beautiful works, and found her to be an extremely multi- talented woman. I contacted her about doing the article."(Bi-weekly Feature Poet - Meena Chopra at postpoems.com)   *- Rachelle Wiegand, poet & a journalist, USA*

"Your writing is emotive and full of romantic expression, very strong. Thank you for your openness."
"White Canvas"   - Deborah Russell, painter and a poet, USA

"I love the vividness in this piece, a combination of Tangible Art and Poetic Art that blends quite nicely".
"Birth Of A Stupor" - Rachelle Wiegand, poet & a journalist, USA

"..perhaps dissolution, emptiness, loss of the walls of concepts, and there by the rebirth of oneness... why? why not? your writing here both real and thought provoking".   *-"Eric Cockrell, USA*

"you are quite a mystery to me. I've been hearing about the quality of your work. I have to say, excellent piece. ...you have an interesting observation with life and the occurrence of events. you're able to draw meaning into the smallest things. A gift."
"Memories In Space" - Dead Poet (Richard Sinclair), USA

"Masterful. Your grasp of subtly explosive imagery is beyond admiration. I found myself holding my breath by the end. Thank you for sharing it.   *"Reverberation"*   *- Stuart Staub, USA*

"You are a beautiful, talented poet and your words are captivating". *"Unbound"*   *- Marianne Chrisos*

"I have to tell you that I am of native American heritage and this is the way that we took care of our dead back in history.. I thought that you did well with this. It was awesome. Thank you for posting this" . *"Pyre"*   *- Renee' Quinn, USA*

"I find your poetry very sensual, and very moving...you have a marvellous talent for touching both the heart, and that inner core of sexuality that brightens the day with thoughts of tender, yet passionate love!!!"   *- HooK USA*

"Dear Meena--I just wanted to tell you how much I've enjoyed reading Ignited Lines--your poetry is wonderful, and I keep your book with my Neruda, Borges, and Rilke collections."
- Robert Darlington, USA

"Dear Ms. Meena Chopra, I viewed a few of your poems on Shadow poetry.com and was very impressed. After reading poems such as "A Glimmer It Was", I can honestly say that you are one of the best poets that I have had the pleasure of reading in a long time. Your words are filled with emotion and depth. Thank you for Sharing your work.
-Nav Chandi, India

Dear Meena, I enjoy your writing. I love meeting people from all over the world. Thanks for being a part of Post Poems. I can't wait to read more of your writing.
-Teresa Jacobs, USA

"Your work expresses a dynamic of power, emotions, and fear. Only a great mind and a multi layered individual could construe the creations that you have set forth. I know I don't know you but through your work, I feel that I do. Your work portrays something more than the picture. It conjures up raw emotion"
-Vique Mora, USA

Meena Chopra is an internationally known award-winning
poet & visual artist with an unbridled passion for words, space,
colours and forms. She has been practicing her arts (Poetry and
Visual Arts) for over three decades now.

Born and brought up in Nainital, India, now lives in Toronto,
Canada. Meena graduated from Isabella Thoburn College
Lucknow. Later qualified as a designer from Delhi and then as
an Artist Educator from RCM Ontario. After having a career
as a designer for seven years in the fashion and garment
industry in India, later switched to fine arts & writing poetry.
She simultaneously entrepreneured in advertising, marketing
and media. She writes poetry both in English and her native
language Hindi and has authored two poetry books. 'SHE! The
Restless Streak' is her third collection which showcases both
her poetry and art.

Her poetry has been translated into German and Urdu as well.

Website: <ins>www.meenachopra-artist.com</ins>